Whispers of the Ineffable
on the threshold of the unspeakable

Other works by Dr. Bishop
*Wisdom of the Animals: A Nature-led Journey into the
Heart of Transformational Leadership*

For more information, visit: www.67happydog.com

First edition, 2021.
ISBN 978-0-5787-9263-7

Acknowledgements:

Thanks to the many friends, teachers, students, and strangers who have helped me along the way. I've learned from countless people in a variety of disciplines across all cultures and wisdom traditions.

I'd like to extend special thanks to Fr. Richard Rohr, Dr. James Finley, Rev. Dr. Cynthia Bourgeault, Dr. Brené Brown, and Ken Wilber for their work. At different times and for different reasons, you've each given me a place to land and a trustworthy path to follow. *Forever grateful.*

Thank you, Tim. You've done it again. Your expertise and intelligence has taken my work to a whole new level. I appreciate you...beyond words.

Dedication

To the most important women in my life.

To Mom,
who formed and nurtured my heart.

To my daughter Carlie,
who opened my heart to love again.

To my wife Paulie,
whose heart became intertwined with mine.

To *Great Love* for catching me in your embrace
when I was lost and falling.
Who knew I was falling for you?

Breaking open to
Whispers of the Ineffable...

It was an unusually bright, crisp, and cool Sunday
evening in March 2006. Sundown sunbeams
poured through the window in the bedroom of
my newly purchased home as a newly single man.
Random items were scattered about, some still in
moving boxes. I'd just dropped off my nine-year-old
daughter at her mother's and found myself sitting on
the edge of my bed, utterly alone. My body fell in
on itself, becoming small, withering into a hunched
bow, my head in my hands. Divorced. Disgraced.
Disheartened. Joined in defeat by the broken hearts
and homes of ones I loved, and others I'd never met.
No one to blame, but myself.

In the paradoxical brightness of the sunset, this
became my darkest hour. Despair arose within like
a separate entity. It overtook me. This gloom was
a creature born and nurtured by my own shadow
side. Its shade of deep loss engulfed me. I clutched
and clung to the pillow like an abandoned child,
while my body twisted and collapsed in on itself. I
wept... madly, wildly, violently. My cries so heavy, it

In the paradoxical brightness of the sunset, this became my darkest hour.

felt like drowning. After each wail, I literally gasped for air. Over and over, it hit me. A gut-wrenching punch, like waves crashing against the solid rock of my fabricated identity. In this moment, an emotional damn burst forth and tears flowed from a pent-up drought of more than sixteen years. The tsunami of grief continued until dusk turned dark. I laid empty and exhausted into the deep night, until slowly, something else stirred.

After thoroughly surrendering to the torment of my suffering, I found myself falling through the despair, like passing through a veil. It wasn't that despair disappeared. It was still there, but somehow muted, softer, and quieter. In the silence, another knowing emerged. A heart-knowing, beyond words. The sense was vast, deep, and unmovable, like I had fallen

In the silence, another
knowing emerged.
A heart-knowing,
beyond words.

through the darkness into a warm embrace, into *Great Love*. This sensation was not sticky, sweet, or shallow, but foundational; a rock-solid framework without judgement or reproach. This gentle holding and powerful embrace drew me in, closer than my own breath, whispering without words, "I've got you, and you are mine." I rested, experiencing a vast peace and steadfast love beyond what my mind could understand, but my heart knew to be true. My faults and failings had not disappeared; they simply lost the power to define who I am.

Since experiencing this dark night, my connection with *Great Love* has remained, fostering a desire for more depth. At times, this connection escaped me. Other times, it completely engulfed me. The pattern became: gaining it and losing it, only to gain and lose it again.

In the summer of 2013, something magical happened that changed the game. I was vacationing in Colorado with my teenage daughter. She overslept, allowing me alone time in the bustling hotel lobby. On a whim, I pulled out my notebook and put pencil to paper. As if lighting was striking my brain, illumination burst forth! My pencil echoed in reverberation of things known only in the heart space of *Great Love*. I couldn't stop. I was in a flow where time and space seemed ancillary. In this first session, I wrote at least six poems. Over the next several years, inspiration came and went, sometimes striking with a startling outpouring of heart wisdom. Afterwards, I would read the words

This gentle holding and powerful embrace drew me in, closer than my own breath…

and muse, "*Where did that come from?*" It still amazes me. These sixty three poems are the result of those sessions that I affectionately call, "taking divine dictation," received like whispers of the ineffable on the threshold of the unspeakable.

About this book... these poems are not in chronological order. In preparing this material, I completed a basic content analysis, sorting poems into "like themes," inviting the reader to traverse a paradoxical process of knowing. Each section is unique, offering glimpses into different levels of connection with the *Beautiful One*. This progression is briefly explained at the beginning of each section, but I prefer it to be mostly experiential.

My faults and failings had not disappeared; they simply lost the power to define who I am.

Perhaps the overarching theme is best summed up in the enduring wisdom prayer of St. Francis of Assisi, *"Make me a channel of your peace."*

Enjoy, my friends!
In *Great Love*,

Patrick

"If I told you the truth about God,
you might think I was an idiot.

If I lied to you about the Beautiful One
you might parade me through the streets shouting,
'This guy is a genius!'"

— Kabir

"Still what I want in my life
is to be willing
to be dazzled
to cast aside the weight of facts
and maybe even
to float a little
above this difficult world."

— Mary Oliver

PART ONE

WHISPERS of the Ineffable

We begin at the beginning. The same place divine knowing begins with us, in what might be considered the "ordinary" and "mundane" of life (which are, of course, anything but). The waves. The reeds. The crayfish. Trees, birds, fire, and friends. The beautiful and ugly are labels we place on the things because we have forgotten we are all one. And yet, our *Beautiful One* still calls us to come home and be dazzled. These manifestations of divine into form are completely and utterly "whispers" of the *Great Love* that inhales and exhales our very existence. But like droplets in the ocean, we are unaware of the vast body of benevolence that holds us in its great embrace because it is everywhere and everything, showing up as, just this.

WAVES

The waves dance on the lake's surface
happy to reflect the sun,
tossing its rays back and forth
in a great game of catch.

They approach me,
splashing a welcome as they roll by,
drawn by a force
to move on,
in a rhythmic dance with glistening partners
who rise with the other's falling.

Gliding by, they seem to
smile and wave
like mythological creatures
seducing me to join them,
or lulling me into
a happy trance.

Reeds

The reeds sway as the winds blow.
No mind for the lightness
of the breeze, or the heaviness of the gale.
They bend however far is necessary.

It is true.
Sometimes one is broken or trampled.
There is no message in that,
other than its brokenness.

It is true.
Some seem to dance in the sun
and glow with the morning dew,
but those are our memories.
Good as that may be,
there is no message in that,
other than its glow.

The brokenness, dance, and glow,
are beyond,
without words, without knowing.
Within a heart space,
the message is clear.
The reeds sway as the winds blow.

Flickering Flame

The fire rises,
always rising, seeking its highest point.
Higher, always higher!

A flickering flame.
A moment in time.
Flashing upward like a dance with now.
Always rising!

The flame doesn't hesitate and
wonder, doubt, or fret,
"Should I go higher?"
No. It flashes and strikes out.
Now, now, now…
Always now.
Taking whatever the moment gives.

Even as it fades
there is no boasting of past flames,
or regrets of lost heights.
Always ready to dance with the now
and take the highest point
the moment gives.

Calling of the Cardinals

I want to write a song,
but I'm not gifted that way.
It is random and elusive to me.

Looking up from my desk,
the cardinal sits alone;
bright red beside black asphalt, white snow.
He pecks seeds offered by my neighbor.

The female hops to a branch
in front of my window.
She looks plump and happy,
faded blushing brown,
watching over her fire-red partner.

In a split second,
they dash away, flashing fey,
scarlet-brown blurred in the brush
something signifying a momentary rush.

Although I didn't hear them,
the heart echoed a fading call, as if
they were singing my song.
A reminder to be on my way.

BROTHER TREE

How strong the tree must be!
To stand so tall,
and yet it is not much thicker than me.
It reaches up to blue sky, golden sun.
Arms in a victory pose.
The wind moves it back and forth,
swaying, playing.

How incredible! Truly.

This tree, covered with skin of bark,
roots long and deep as branches are high,
lifting water for nourishment,
working against gravity,
buds ready to pop and capture
the raw energy of the sun
and return to us the very air we breathe.

How can our response be anything less than awe?
Unless we are asleep.

CRAYFISH

Do you remember the little boy?
He'd hunt crayfish for hours using a technique
perfected over endless summer days.
Moving ever so slowly,
leaving the sandy bottom undisturbed.
Creeping, patiently, step by painfully slow step,
until hunched over a flat rock,
gently lifting in anticipation.
"There's one!" he'd excitedly proclaim.
Never looking up.
Never letting the crayfish leave his sight.
Slowly, dipping the plastic pail
behind the tiny crustacean,
using his other hand to scare it backward.
He scoops, shouting triumphantly, "I got it!"
Ready to show anyone, everyone
this amazing alien living just beyond his front yard,
with its black beady eyes, long antennae,
surprisingly strong claws, and mini lobster-like tail.
I remember this boy, enchanted in this simple quest,
entertained beyond time because it didn't matter
if his back was sunburned,
or he forgot to eat, or he looked silly.
All that mattered was the adventure and exploration
and connection to the awe that was,
the crayfish.

One Leaf

The one leaf
withered and dying
will rot and wash away
only knowing this hill, this boulder, this tree.
The ants will use it as a home
for only a short while
before the rain, ice, and snow
return her to the earth.
Once she was vibrant gold, red, or orange
creating the autumn palate with billions
of brothers and sisters.
Before that, she was green and supple
fresh and alive, moist and firm,
changing the very air with her very life.
Before that, she was a bud.
A cluster of cells with great potential
ready to burst forth.
Way before that, she was part of
Mother Earth,
as she is now and was throughout,
none different, but in name and service.

Mountain Ferns

I sit in the mountains
waiting for what I do not know,
and knowing it is already here.
An old spider web winks in and out
of existence when illuminated by the sun,
then falling back in shadow.
It has a message for me.

The breeze moves the ferns back and forth
more and more, making its presence known,
then gently relaxing, subsiding like a wave.
It has a message for me.

Shadows dance on the large boulder
I have claimed as my seat.
Somewhere light is received
creating the dancer and the dance.
They are everywhere!
Filling the forest with twirling leaves
silhouetted by swirling shadows of the original.

Both are real, but
one creates the other
only when bathed in light.
In darkness, both are lost.

Winter Day

Grey skies cloud my mind.
Bare branches hang lifeless
framed by dirty windows with winter residue.
The chill is enough to cause retreat
in slow, lethargic ways.
Burnt orange pine needles
dropped months ago, in late fall,
find places to gather.
Huddled by cold winds, melting snow, hard rains.
Some resist, getting stuck
wherever they can plant their pointedness.
The flappable female cardinal is a pale reminder
that life goes on.
She finds a way
to do what must be done,
giving me courage and strength
to do the same.

Dankook Mountain

The writing threatens to disturb
what cannot be said,
daring to encroach on the unspeakable.

I sit in silence, but it is not quiet.
Twigs break. Leaves rustle. Cicadas buzz.
Squirrels chirp. Birds call.
Unseen nature drops from the canopy of trees.
A walking stick falls from somewhere,
landing feet from my feet.
Awkward in its sporadic movements.

I breathe. Quiet the mind.
Feeling the boulder that invited me to sit.
Watching the ants and tiny red spiders
working so hard,
as butterflies dart by.

The sun is a spotlight
highlighting different scenes every time
it breaks through
inviting me to
dance with now.

WINDSONG

What whispers in the wind for you?
Promises of dreams
and hope-filled aspirations?
Lost love and time gone by?
Or does it carry something else?

A kiss from someone unknown.
A seed yet to be planted and sown.
A delight of cool breeze.
A floating leaf letting go of home.
Another breath from your creator.

To hear is to know
that the windsong is
the same as the exhale of heaven
waiting for you to take it all in.

CHESTNUT TREE

I found a chestnut today.
It had a story to tell
about how it happened to be there,
how it fell.
As I listened,
there was also a song in the tree
about the letting go of something special
because it was time.
They were the same song and story,
but different for each,
and both were true.

LITTLE GIRL

You are grown and growing.
The same and ever changing.
Static now, always dynamic.

I see glimpses of me in you.
Shy, reserved, unsure and
unwilling to stand out, yet
bold, happy, eyes on the future
filled with promise.

A flash of passion for what you love.
A sleepiness when disengaged.
Trying to balance independence and duty,
knowing and being.
A struggle I understand all too well

You're so much farther than I ever was.
A maturity beyond your years,
and it amazes me.
I have no greater joy than watching you,
grown and growing.
Finding yourself on this path that is yours.
Filling my heart with
a father's love for his little girl.

Old Friend

The memory is foggy, old friend.
Times of late-teens
on warm summer nights
sipping champagne from tiny bottles;
our reward for a long day of work
at a place where the other half knew how to live.
And we'd dream. And we'd match wits.
And we'd pontificate. And we'd wonder,
while bubbles loosed our lips
and water's beauty inspired young hearts.
Innocent, when ignorance was bliss.
The *richness* of those days
dissolved into my being
where it mixed with my marrow
becoming part of my blood and bones
changing forever
my view of the world,
reflecting the nature of the divine,
the nature of now, the nature of then.
Great Love. Great Loss.
Still, I thank you.
These were the days of my early awakening.
A first glimpse of freedom
found in the safety of one
I will forever call, old friend.

Steadfast & True

Steadiness has its own reward.
Covered in mundane,
it grinds through,
consistency its blade,
forged in perseverance,
and the desire to outlast.
Like water wearing down granite,
time is the only consideration.
Who can know the speed or rate?
It does not matter.
The one who is steadfast
completes the task
one moment by one moment,
content in knowing
greatness is not earned in one move,
but by repeated attention to this one,
this one, this one, and… this one,
until mediocrity crumbles under the
resolve of a dogged determination to
meet the challenge of this moment
with an outrageously ordinary consistency
until all is done.

Stories Untold

The book shop is full
with people who sit alone, wanting to connect.
Sipping their Starbucks,
flipping through magazines they don't buy,
drawn here not just by the books.
They (we), clearly need to be with others.
The elderly seem to know better.
There is a group of women knitting,
while old men play cribbage.
How did this place become their social hangout?
What does it say about me that I find it odd?

The stories in the books that fill the shelves
are as dead as the hearts of the lonely,
waiting for a kind, curious soul to pick them up
and lovingly go through
and read the story of a nondescript title.
Their unread pages depicting
failure, not enough, suffering.
They've written and
read their own stories too often.
They've forgotten its authorship,
settling for the first story that wrote itself down.

The Tavern

So strange.
Sitting in a crowed bar, alone.
I grab my chin, a nervous habit.
I notice, rubbing fingers against three-day stubble,
to release tension, I suppose.
To appear academic?
To see if I'm still here.
Laughter rises from a high-top table of single women,
followed by a "crack!" of hands clapping,
an exclamation point on their conversation.
A young couple sits at the bar
lost in each other's stories.
The elderly couple next to me
cover the events of the week.
People flow in and out of the foyer,
like busy ants or worker bees,
fulfilling duties of an unseen queen.
My eyes keep getting drawn to the TV screen,
the best defense for a man alone.
The bartender skips behind his counter
with a stack of bills and a large grin.
And the piano in the corner sits empty
with so many potential songs
if only my heart could play.

Dreadlocks

My dreadlocks are dirty.
My piercings turn you off.
The love-lost meaning of my
sleeve-tattoo
is empty in your surface-level shallowness.

Are you in touch with your body?
I don't hate mine.
I feel everything.
Depth is my language.
Pain my unique dialect.
And beauty shows up as the
wardrobe of the world.

I'm ready to share it all with you,
except...
You see me as unworthy.
Image is all you take in.
I understand.
It's my protection,
to warn those who feign interest.

But, if you'd ask, feel, reach, drop your gaze,
you'd see me.
Broken, but real. Lost in myself.
Hopeful; more than I appear.
Then, maybe you'd see,
I'm just like you.

Path to Awakening

I pass them by,
swerving a bit to avoid them,
listening to *"Jesus and Buddha"* and
cruising a comfortable fifty-eight.
They turn towards me, thumbs extended.
I'm caught.

They are older, rougher, scarier
than I'd like.
Mid-50s, unshaven, goatee, ponytail,
loose fitting denim shirt, beat up jeans,
bad teeth, bad breath, smell like smoke.
Will he get my car dirty? Will he try to rob me?
Where's the damsel in distress?
I curse, bite my lip, and pull over.

He explains,
ran out of gas,
a few miles from home,
I'll grab my truck and a gas can.
Thanks for stopping.

It cost me nothing.
Not even 100 yards out of my way.
Such a simple act.
I return to my audio program,
"Paths to awakening,
finding the four noble truths in the heart of the gospel."

Love Language .

My poems become old friends over time.
Well-worn words of intimate relations
with him unknown to me,
until he shows up here.
Often tentative and unsure, but
always vulnerable.

I reread them like trying on old clothes.
The new ones don't fit as well,
but if I give them time and
open to them,
they show me their comfort and depth
in shades and hues I had forgotten.

Maya says words are things.
I believe that.
They are my love language
and when I write without reservation
my words flow,
revealing and healing,
locked up pieces of my heart and soul,
letting their ugly, beautiful secrets out
so I can love them, myself, and then,
gently returning them,
wrapped in a spirit of humility.
The fertile soil of self-love,
making it easier and even more lovely
next time.

The Dance

This is so cathartic,
and vain.
Why would I think anyone
would want to hear what I have to say?
What I write?

These poems.
The musings of my heart, my soul.
They flow out from me.
Me. Not me.
From somewhere else.
I watch the pencil pour,
like taking divine dictation,
the words flow, filling the page.

They are a release, I suppose.
A place in time. A letting go.
I'd lie if I said
I didn't want you to like them.
And yet, I also know,
they are not mine.

This is my dance of ego.
This is my spirit song.

"If all the forgiveness the heavens have known
could be offered from one face,
would you accept that divine pardon?"

— St. Francis of Assisi

PART TWO

Whispers OF THE Ineffable

It's called "liminal space." The place in between
where the rational critical mind learns to loosen
its grip and become something more. Tell me
something you're absolutely certain about.
Your name? Your beliefs? Your body, emotions,
or thoughts? Yes, and… no. The seer is not
the seen. Explain death. Tell me about love.
Why does she suffer? Why can't he be free of
pain? Where does the path of the Dark Night
lead if not a place of surrender? In this stage
of the journey, we are shaken and stirred by
the realization that we are not in control. We
are not this perfectly constructed mass of ego
identity we've built for ourselves. The walls of
certainty begin to crack. Stay. Don't run. Don't
try to escape. Let go. Sit with it. Breathe into
it. Hold it. Allow the falling. Over and over; the
death of a thousand cuts. You will find yourself
held in a cloud of unknowing where a new
paradigm begins to form.

BREAKING OPEN

I want to cry.
For, or at what, I don't know,
but it overcomes me at times.
And I love it.

Because somehow, I know
it is breaking me open,
breaking my heart,
making more room for love,
for compassion, for patience,
for now, for sad joy, for peace.

And this is desperately
who I want to become.
Or maybe, this is who I already am
and this weeping is a stripping away.

Either way,
I like it.
I look forward to losing myself
in its embrace
again and again.
Until, I am more it than me.

PENDULUM

It scares me.
I don't want to swing
like the pendulum, from love to hate.

When I'm a place for love
it is a beautiful thing,
as if I can see love in everything.

Then, I wake up (or do I sleep?),
and I swing... almost as if I have to.
Is it to offset such love?
To satisfy the ego?
Human nature?

I hate the driver who just cut me off.
The toothpaste squirting on the sink.
The stubbed toe.
How stupid can I be?
How careless can she be?
So inconsiderate!

I hear myself.
How "Enlighted!" What "Grace!"
I'm doing it again.
Breath. Let go. Forgive. Love.

The pendulum shifts again,
a bit softer and slower than before.

The Desert

The desert is always
a place of letting go,
isolation, subtraction, suffering.

It is where the Jewish people were born
and wandered lost.
It is where Jesus was tempted.
A time of fasting and prayer.
Did you know Muhammad went there?
So did the Buddha, Confucius, and Lao Tzu.
Have you been there?
On the edge of society,
where no one willingly wants to go?

I suspect we've all made
a pilgrimage in our own way.
How far in and out doesn't matter
as much as how often.
Because you die a little for every visit.
A good death.
A death to the small self.
A stripping away
and after a while
it feels more like
a calling, an appeal, an invitation.

The emptiness fills you
unlike all the life you've known before.
Less breadth, less width, but endless depth,
in a singular point that is you.

And all I can do is sink,
as if passing through
the desert sands of an hourglass,
dropping into a resting place
within and without.

LATE NIGHT LONELY

Late night lonely fills my soul
with ghosts of time gone by.
Foggy images, fuzzy sounds
drift in and out of memory.
Each one carrying different flavors,
all leading right back to
late night lonely.
As if to remind me
the cost of past sins,
the loss found in the emptiness
of hollow dreams
once held high as banners
declaring foolishness yet to be discovered.
Only now realizing
the futility of running blind
into the dark night.

THE GAP

Where is the life for the second half of life?
It feels like death.
Dull. Bland. Vanilla. Blah.
I weep and long for
the certainty of the first half.
I knew what to do.
I knew who I was.
Goals were clear:
Power. Position. Money.
Easy targets. Now what?
I could write the next goal, but why?
What's the point?
They no longer excite me.
Part of me is sad, missing the trajectory of success.
A Pleasantville of limbo is my residence.
Nowhere to go, but to follow the path of doubt.
It's an oddity of this place,
wondering if I'll break through
to taste the sweetness of this moment
because there seems to be an
intuitive difference between knowing
you're being served and enjoying the first bite.

Lessons Learned

"*They're hunted for sport,*" she said.
"*Brought here from Europe…*
mountain goats aren't indigenous."
(They don't even know how to spell it.)

Confusion crept and lingered
across the face of the little boy.
"*What's sport?*" he asked.

"*For fun,*" the nature guide replied.
"*They're killed for fun.*"

"*Oh,*" was his soft reply.
A part of his soul dies with a whimper,
unnoticed.

Wwjd

Jack says,
"Be a worm.
Long for nothing.
Attain everything."
Sounds like something he'd say.

Frustration

My spirit runs dry.
Where have you gone, my Lord?
Where has the life leaked away to?
Lost. Even my pencil has drained of its fullness.
I wander in circles in the sand.
No. Not even circles. That would be too precise.
My wandering is absent any direction.
As if, after each step,
my lost-ness is renewed
and my next step has no
relationship to the one I just took.
Indecisive. Paralyzed by unknowing.
My heart longs for motivation, inspiration
focus, direction, clarity.
My mind is a cobweb of conflicting ideas.
A pit of jumbled brilliance
which I'm unable to piece together.
My failings seem trivial.
Even they don't affect my livelihood.
Beyond depression or despair, is frustration.
Raw and true.
Not knowing who I am.
What I'm to do.
What my step is to be.
And so,
I don't move at all.

Longing

My heart wants.
A memory of what it knows it has lost
long ago in separation of divine into form.
Unable to go back and reconnect.
Unable to find you in wanting,
although I've tried
numerous times in a multitude of ways.
Distracting? Yes.
Fulfilling? No.
It only makes the emptiness bigger, deeper.

I'm told "now" holds the answer: the holy grail!
But that's only partially true,
because old remnants of loss are always there.
I hold the pieces in silence
as a reminder of my home,
how far I've come and yet to go.
I will never see it with these eyes,
and so my prayer is that I learn more and more
to let you see through me.

A Necessary Wound

He touches this place,
knowing it is a sacred wound of the living,
of loving too greatly.
The fire of desire burns in too much intensity.

Time has softened the pain,
but it is deep, full of sorrow and regret.
Only by allowing, admitting, holding
does it lose some sting,
breaking open places closed and lost,
like healing ointment, cleaning the wound
allowing new growth
of forgiveness and compassion.

From time to time
a cleansing must occur, keeping it tender,
so as not to scar over and become hard.
A choice to be open or closed.
To share the suffering of humanity.
It remains as a reminder. A necessary wound.
A right of passage to *Great Love*.
A requirement to live in God's heart.

Homecoming

Darkness, he covers me.
Silence, she comes to me.
Lost in the vastness of their embrace,
I am coming home.

Somewhere between the shadowland
and the place I know
is the one I love.
Never gone. Always here. Ever present.

Calling me and waiting for my return
falling in laughter and joy.
My heart is one with
him unknown to me,
her unknown to me.

Confusion floods in with "understanding mind"
because she says, there is no understanding
because he says, you can only unknow to know.

I breathe and ask for allowing
giving permission to all I am
to let go, to surrender and,
go with these ones I love.

DEMONIZED

Why is the sound of
the dump truck, ugly?
And the sound of
the cardinal, beauty?
Who decides such things?

Why do we always cheer for life
when death holds the key?
The spider, the wolf, the rat,
the snake, the lizard, and the ant
must also survive, yet
they are given our sins
and labeled dirty, unworthy, evil.
They are no less than
the dove, butterfly, and goldfish.
Our naming makes it so.

Life is a beautiful tragedy.
All we are given
is everything we should
accept and embrace,
inhaling its given-ness fully,
until we have to exhale, and
learn to let go.

Science? Religion? Beyond.

Science can explain almost any phenomenon:
Why a candle burns.
How food becomes energy.
Where the Monarch flies.
But when I watch a candle,
I don't understand... I do *not* understand.
The birth of a baby,
a flower opening to sunshine, or even
a kitten purring.

Religion claims to explain the divine:
Peace. Faith. Love.
But peace passes all understanding.
Faith is moving forward in darkness.
Love is the very nature of the ineffable.
I don't understand... I do *not* understand.

My response is awe.
My response is amazement.
No explanation.

Just because we name it doesn't make it known.
And yet, somewhere beyond, all can be known.

The Mountain Buddha

One says,
"*Stupid. Worthless.*
Wasted time, wasted space, wasted place.
Who do you think you are?"

Quietly, the other replies,
"*Sorry, I know.*
I'm nobody. Life sucks. Fuck it all.
What's the point?"

A third chuckles,
fancies himself, "The Observer."
Maybe he is. Or maybe,
just a softer version of the one.

A breath in and out
reveals a home for all to rest.

I imagine.
A cave on the side of a mountain
with a ledge and room enough
to pace, to face the world.

I stand there.
A view to open spaces
comforted by the massive rock at my back.
The mouth of the cave invites me to sit,
and I do,
pretending to be the Buddha
and somehow, there's peace in that.

ANXIETY

Vigilance is always there,
like a high frequency sound only I can hear.
Or an incessant buzzing.
White noise on the edge of consciousness,
growing in intensity
in times of doubt or stress,
like fuel on a fire.

Over the years it's become
more like a cantankerous lover,
some of its urgency gone,
or diffused,
or not all that important,
or I've loosened my grip,
or its grip has loosened me.

Still, it's familiar in an odd way
and I've grown accustomed to its presence.
In better moments, I hold it, feed it love.
In worse moments, it sucks on fear and avoidance.

This paper tiger calls mind its home
as it stalks my heart
echoing deep roaring fear in
the caverns of my belly
until the calls reverberate to my soul
absorbed
in the ground of your being;
the love you have made of me.

My Little Demon

Sitting in the spotlight.

My little demon
ascended from the depths of somewhere
where it had been fed and nurtured
by the shadow side of great lies.

My little demon
lured in by so many eyes on me
13 pairs; 26.
The chemical reaction.
I've studied it for years.
I know how it works.
Knowledge isn't power in this case.
It terrifies me.

My little demon
rides its dragon of downward death spiral.
Normal speaking becomes not so normal.
This lip, the one that's been mine my whole life,
begins to quiver.
I silent scream for it to stop,
but it's no longer mine to control.

My little demon!
I am drowning in fear.

Return

The wheel of life is turning.
What seemed stagnant and still for so long
has broken free of the hold,
setting in motion inevitable change.
I am allowing and even welcome
the shift of momentum.
I have tried to be steady and loyal so long,
preparing for this exact moment,
lining it all up like dominoes.
Now they are falling, one after another.
With each drop, an excitement and anticipation
of the next to go.
In no bad way, it has felt like
holding back a wall of water, a tsunami,
by brute force of will.
Staying the course, paying the price,
serving my penance,
happy to do so as it is my responsibility,
and yet, knowing it is beginning to fall.
In the resistance is my power
which will soon be released and
free to flow where it will
and my conditioning will allow
me the strength to ride it
to my love, my heart's desire.

LETTING GO

I must fall
open armed, eyes closed
in that space and place
where I am.

I must fall
without hope of being caught
but knowing I am sustained
in the descent.

There is no other thing to do.
Nowhere else to go.
No idea so important it must be thought.
No feeling so real it must be felt.

Past regrets fade; fantasies abate.
There is nothing.
A continuous surrender
to an ever deeper falling.

Live Through Me

Everything has the soul of God,
not that we can know what that means.
It is a heart knowing.
It is a gut knowing.
It is an unknowing,
of the unspeakable and ineffable.

And yet,
when heard in still, small places
it becomes
a rock of certitude.
Humbly known beyond knowing.
Given by love.
Given by beauty.
By truth, by beyond.

All I can do is say, "Yes!"
And weep in gratitude,
in sorrow, in hope,
surrendering and praying,
begging, crying out, trusting
that this love will somehow
live through me.

My Plea

Who is my brother?
Some serve by loving
things of this earth.
Some take care of the
hungry, homeless, and hurting.
Some protect the children
and mentally disabled.

Who is my sister?
Some pray for those at war.
Others help the wounded soldier
or the violated woman.
Some help the single mom
or forgotten men in prison.

Who is mine to love,
for no other reason than
to serve,
and to touch the many faces of God?
Will you send me your sheep?
Will you show me your needs
that I can uniquely fill?
Will you help me be ready?
I want to be ready.
Here I am.

"One day
He did not leave
after kissing me."

— Rabia

PART THREE

Whispers of the INEFFABLE

Who or what is this ineffable? Infinitely
knowable divine, yet unnamable. Still, we try.
*Great Love. One Taste. Beautiful One. Divine
Embrace.* St. John of the Cross said, imagine
describing the color yellow to a blind man.
What words could you use? None suffice. So
it is with God. St. John says trying to name
the divine is like trying to put the ocean into
a thimble. Jewish wisdom teachers used only
the breath (YH-inhale; WH-exhale). Lao Tzu
says the Tao that can be named is not the real
Tao. God cannot be known with the mind,
yet is infinitely knowable in ways beyond
knowing. Paradox. A new paradigm.
The still small voice. The eternity of now.
The depth of the heart space. These poems
are expressions of desire that always fall short,
yet still call forth deep unto deep, like unto
like. As my teacher, James Finley says, these
are words in the service of what cannot
be said… whispers of the ineffable on the
threshold of the unspeakable.

CREATION

It is said,
when God created this world
it was an act of pure love
giving itself away
as creation.

Love willingly
shattered itself
into a multitude of countless sparks,
setting in motion
the divine dynamic
manifestation of itself
into form.

Given flow.
Always present.

SPARK

You are more than you realize.
Someday, your beauty will fade.
Your intellect will faulter.
Your money will fail to fulfill your desire.
At that moment, will you know you are more?

Your heart longs to share its love.
Your soul's desire is to connect.
The fire from beyond would ignite your world.
All it requires is a small gesture,
and all the courage you can offer.
Its spark is your "Yes!" in this moment.

Birds of Saint Francis

What did St. Francis say to the birds?

You are beautiful!
Look at your exquisite feathers, so full and light
with just the right color
to hide you in the wild brush.
They allow the air to float beneath
and the water to roll off above,
warming your soft body in the winter,
falling off in spring to help make your baby's bed.
That would be quite enough, yet there is more!
Your voice is music and light and life to my ears.
Sing to me the simple joys of your days and nights.
Song on wings, raised high for all to hear.
You are God's very tenderness
allowed to voice his love
and fly to places far and wide
to be witness to delicate, sweet love
taken care of in all ways.

The birds embraced the words of St. Francis.
His voice carried a song of their shared essence.

Springtime of My Soul

I can sit, eyes closed,
face raised to meet you, my sun,
drinking in your warmth,
like a stranger finding home for the first time.
Your rays, like millions of tiny keys
unlocking secret seeds of contentment
planted along my skin
waiting in anticipation for your special touch
opening and bursting forth in
a wild and mad freedom of
joy, love, deep gratification
along, over, throughout my body
to places winter made me forget
soaking in deeper
until the warmth of your gaze
merges with the fire of my desire
melting and mixing in coexistence
making us one, and once again awakening
the springtime of my soul.

LEAF SONG

The leaf cannot sing by itself.
She sits, waits, grows
perched in readiness
with brothers and sisters
prepared for the sun,
this bird, that fly, an ant or inchworm.
All are welcome!

From a place unknown to her
a movement begins.
Giddy with delight, she dances,
never sure of the next motion
but open to any direction.

Her siblings join in the same way
creating a synchronized ballet that
spreads throughout the tree
from leaf to leaf to branch to limb.
An unseen gust awakens a voice
sung together through the intimate dance
of an unseen lover
whose touch resonates the beingness
of all who allow the movement,
of all who allow the song.

Graves of Gethsemani

I walk through the valley of dead,
tombstones lined on both sides.
Names and dates fifteen decades gone.
No longer a home of the soul.
A place of decayed bodies,
old stories, faded memories,
and a shadow of the work done, lives on.
Their graves are a witness
to a longing for the whispers of the ineffable.
A desire to know and be known
by our creator.
One source through, with, in, is, was, and yet to be.
Old hearts, like Merton's, give testimony
that I is in i.
Drawn together, magnets to steel.
Lives of dedication to
animal hunger of our being
to be reunited
even as we ourselves
come to understand
I&i is what is.

Lived Beauty

I can show you what it means
to be beautiful.
It is a persistence of the heart
to forgive
to look for good
to hold pain
to share suffering.

Beauty comes from dark places
bubbling up with hope
in the knowledge
that we're all one,
that there's only love.

Beauty shows up
in the tenacity to do what's right
versus what's easy.

It arrives when you're clinging
to the final fine threads of patience,
holding the anger, rage, and frustration,
and not reacting to it, but
breathing through

and finding yourself
on the other side
where it's all okay, and
crying because you're thankful
to be there
and wondering at the grace
that brought you through
and knowing, this exact moment
is where we're meant to live.

I am Animal Spirit

The blackbird rides the wind
not for the thrill of flight, but for food.
The bee floats the flowers
ignoring their beauty, fulfilling an unknown drive.
The robin finds a worm
taste aside, providing a meal for its fledgling.

I too, am animal, yet, more.
I sense my body and its needs.
Instinct wants, yet mind can intercede.
Passion can overrule, spirit can overcome.
Ego can manifest in all,
or dissolve into the background.

Being human is animal, rational, divine.
A confusing state of multiplicity
the wild don't seem to struggle against.
For you and I,
the path seems to be
simply to walk,
love the animal,
know the truth,
allow divine to shine through in all aspects.

Healing Place

We all suffer
The extent and duration differ
Life is lived in the way we respond
Hearts broken open
Hearts closed off

Sadness and isolation
The heart shrivels into itself
Like a grape becoming a raisin
Grasping for love it doesn't hold
A self-inflicted wound

Falling
Into the perceived weakness of losing
What we don't own
In courage
Allowing the hurt to affect the heart
To soften, to surrender, to be vulnerable
To be naked in spirit to what is

There, we are held
In our precious imperfection
In a love smitten with our frailty
When you've been there,
you will know

Now Here

There is no place you are not.
If I show up,
you are there!

You are easiest to see
in the places we all love:
sunsets, rocky mountain highs,
the duck, deer, and wild turkey,
raging storms and crickets.
Unfiltered flow.

But what really blows me away
is that you are here,
in this hotel lobby
among the registration chatter,
the phone calls, and smooth jazz,
the paisley carpet, marble columns,
Internet access and Starbucks.

They are distractions,
if I allow it.
They are paths to you,
if I allow it.
If I show up, you are here.

NOW'S RAZORED EDGE

Where does the rush of day come from?
And the buzz of night?
Fed by our own insatiable appetite
for more, more, much more!

The mind dances on either side
of now's razored edge,
back and forth,
never finding the deep peace
in the sliver sharpness
of elusive now.

Banging ourselves against its edge
we are chaffed, unknowing
(as it is the only way we know).
Too close to see its life.
We don't recognize its brilliance
because it is disguised as boredom,
and not enough.
Yet, it is all in all.

This Lived Moment

Inhaling… I wonder if the room has less air.
Exhaling… I wonder if the world also expanded.

Contemplating our collective breathing
I'm made aware how alive this world is.
Yet, it is more than breath.

The flag waves in the wind,
so mundane, but new eyes see its miracle.
Symbolic dynamics of form.
Constantly changing; never the same
from moment to moment
(echoes of forever reverberate).

Flickering flames reach higher.
Trickling waters descend lower.
Birth. Breath. Growth. Death.

We are witnesses.
We are living examples.
The dynamic nature of
the infinite moment.
Always here, only now.

TASTE OF THE MOMENT

What do you want yourself to know?
What lies in secret?
What is hidden from view?

Covering unheard mysteries is a fragile ego, who…
Can't hear. Won't hear. Doesn't know how to hear.

Like salt, dissolved in water,
infusing its character
dominating the solution
masked in complexity.
If consumed, this union will not lead to life.

The blending must be gently addressed
through purpose and effort
with cost and discomfort.
Once distinct and differentiated,
both water and salt,
both heart and ego,
give life and flavor,
making known
the refined taste of this moment.

THE NAMING

Who are you?
What was your name
before your parents named you?

Every leaf has a name.
Even the gray wolf is known as
Canin Lupus.
Do you think he knows that?
Why should you be any different?

Should we call him, Jack?
Or her, Diane?
Maybe you know him best as Peter!

What's most interesting to me,
is we try to name God.
What name have you given her?
Is there any name
that captures the ineffable?
I've heard,
it's like putting the ocean into a thimble.

Pick up some dirt.
A pebble.
A yellow dandelion.
A walnut.
Rub it in your hands.
Smell it.
Stare at it,
until it speaks to you.

What does it say
its name is?
What does it say
its mission is?
What's its purpose?

Why should it be any different,
for you?

WEIRD

You have to be willing
to be weird
to really love the *Beautiful One*.
Not prune juice in holy water weird,
in the moment weird.
Willing to take the picture of the flower.
Willing to be okay with silence.
Willing to sit and notice.
And appreciate
the happy dog chasing the ball
the little boy in oversized flip flops
the ant crawling on the paper
the beginner practicing the clarinet
the grown man talking love to his baby

To be in the moment
you have to be weird
and accept whatever it offers
dropping labels
even the ones we give ourselves
(like weird).

ADDICTION

To be more loving
you must focus on love.
Left to my own devices
my ego takes over
and it can be a dark place
of blame, and all things wrong.
It takes an act of conscious choice
to let it go.
Even then, it's like an addiction
to be attached to what makes you miserable.

BLIND FAITH

I don't care
about the labels of your morality.
Christian, Jew, Buddhist, Muslim, Hindu, Zen,
Agnostic, Atheist
mean little to me.

What I want to connect with is
the goodness of your soul,
the tenderness of your heart,
the joy of your being you,
the suffering that breaks you open.

I'm scared of people
who always have the right answer.
Your beliefs don't make you holy.
It is not who you project to me that I love.
My heart resonates with your
fragility, weakness, vulnerability,
and strength of character,
because that's when we're one.

That's when we become the face of God.
That's when we become
the cosmic Christ, the spark, the Buddha,
the mercy, the Atman, the Tao,
the who knows, the nothing.

Faith isn't certitude.
Faith is living with doubt.
Trusting this exact moment,
that your next step in darkness,
is yours to take.
It's holding the pain and loving the question.
It is not faith that moves mountains.
Faith moves me
to appreciate the grand splendor
of the unfathomable mountain
and come to realize
my place is not to move, but to be moved.

Your Story

You have a story to tell.
It is singular, special, all your own.
No one else can tell it,
which is why it's so important you do.

There will be joys and sorrows,
discoveries and lessons learned.
Moments when you felt God,
others when you feel alone.
Tears will fall in the telling
because you are
in the sandbox of the soul
and vulnerability draws
the affection from beyond
into your heart space
where we can barely stand
the love gaze
of that which calls us.

You have a story to tell.
One that connects you to me.
One that reveals our humanity
here and now; specific yet universal.
Your story opens a window
for God to experience her creation.
A space for us to be one.

Reacquaintance

Let me share something
I don't even know myself.
My heart,
sits like mist on a still inland lake,
cool end of summer morning
waiting for your warming rays
to crest forth from the expectant sunrise
to warm me with the hope of the East
like a lover, longing to be filled with you.
The aroma of desire lingers, just out of reach.
I wait in the electricity of anticipation
knowing you're already here.
In the darkness before the dawn,
resonating in my breast,
like a slow and low, steady bass note.
The breeze stirs, playing your melody in time.
I am your captive, enraptured audience of one
ready to be the instrument of your choosing.
Play through me whatever song you desire
because it is your breath,
your love touch
through me
to be moved and played
in our eternal dance of reacquaintance.

INTRODUCTION

I AM alive in i am.
Because you live through me, i am.
In this place, you are everywhere, i am.
Every thing is new.
I see the sun for the first time.
Illuminating tree and trail bed,
skipping off the silent pond,
rustling leaves, crackling sticks.

I walk by, thinking I know what I see.
Because I can name it.
Because I have seen it a million times.
Because I put myself above it.

A closer look creates awe.
Roots form steps, crisscrossing my path
on their way to find water.
A squirrel slowly scuttles by,
stopping steps from me,
head tilting, as if pondering my existence
before lightly skipping on her way.

They remind me,
I do not know them,
because this is our first meeting.

Vulnerability

My naked heart lies before you,
born and lived in the folly
of now in the divine dance.
It's for you to decide which is better,
foolish truths or believable lies?

THE RIVER OF WOLJEONGSA TEMPLE

The green pines stand like a great gentle wall.
They whisper of another
way beyond their prickly branches.

Rushing waters call to me, as do the birds;
a happy, welcoming greeting.
The crickets call.
The squirrels call.
The blackbirds call.
A bumble bee floats nearby, curiously testing
my resolve to accept the untamed wildness.

Flowers dressed
in yellows, whites, purples, reds, and orange
burst forth from deep greens of the mountainside.

Encouraged by the abundance and delight
of their embrace,
I breathe them in.
I hear only them.
I see only them.
I feel only them.

This moment is filled with the sweet taste
of their innocence, being, presence, wakefulness.
Answering their call, I walk among them,
knowing as I do, my "yes" has made us one.
Nature here knows my name.
The river herself invites me to sit on her bank.
Framed by large boulders, she tells me,
"Time is the knife used to carve this rock."

The water glides down the mountain,
like liquid pixies
dancing, laughing, playing, twirling around bends.
Lapping along long logs,
popping over buried stones.
In a dynamically consistent motion,
their giggles heard in gushes and waves,
tumbling over one another.
Some rest in side pools,
slowly finding their way back, seamlessly
reconnecting with watery brothers and sisters.

The river invites my hand.
Open palm, I allow fingers to fall
and feel her cool embrace.
Back and forth, she massages each finger,
closer and gentler than any lover,
more intimate than I have known.
I take what she offers,
bringing her to my lips, face, and hair.
Soothing and cooling, I go back again and again,
until my skin and hair have soaked her in,
becoming part of me.
We sit together in silence.
The moment flickers.
She whispers, "*Goodbye*...."

Tears well up, knowing,
for that twinkling,
we were one.
Wiping my eyes,
I release them back into her flow
where they merge and carry on
to places known to me
only in the shared essence of
the river of Woljeongsa Temple.

Whispers of the INEFFABLE
on the threshold of the unspeakable

About the Author

Patrick Bishop is an author, speaker, and award-winning professor in the College of Business at Ferris State University. In addition to a PhD in Leadership, Bishop is a graduate of the Living School (Center for Action & Contemplation). He holds several distinctions, most notably, Riso-Hudson Enneagram certification.
Whispers of the Ineffable follows the 2020 release of his first book, *Wisdom of the Animals.*

Bishop lives in Grand Rapids, Michigan and offers experiential workshops through his leadership company, Happydog Consulting & Training. He can be reached at www.67happydog.com or 67happydog@gmail.com

Morning Coffee

All I want
is for the *Great Ineffable Lovely One*
to drink my coffee.
Each morning,
I sit in silence
holding my cup
as an offering
an invitation, waiting…
As warmth spreads through open hands,
I breathe,
inhaling dark roast.
Ever so subtly,
a flicker, a glimmer.
Shhhh…*she* arises.
The mug moves to her mouth
tipping tastes to waiting lips
receiving smokey richness
an endless warmth entering me,
sparking awareness
realizing in witnessing
One Taste
is drinking my coffee.

CPSIA information can be obtained
at www.ICGtesting.com
Printed in the USA
BVHW051357281021
620179BV00014B/370